1

Also By Rise' Harrington and Bryan Jameison
(Dorgeck)

Guide Lights - Attune to Your Angels and Spirit Guides - Begin to Heal Your Life and Move Towards Your Soul Purpose

Reincarnation - The Four Factors - Soul Freedom Series Vol 1

Entity Attachment Removal - Self-Help Procedure - The ABC of Releasing Spirit Attachments for Do It Yourselfers -Soul Freedom Series Vol 3

Repelling Demons -
The Loving Way to Heal Ourselves and Our World
Soul Freedom Vol 2

By Rise' Harrington 1953 -
By Bryan Jameison, Regression Therapist 1933 - 2002
(*Aka* Dorgeck, Ascended Master)

Overseeing Authority Idahohl-Adameus
(Aka St. Germain)

Rev 2.3 07/03/2023

KDP ISBN: 9781708761547

The purpose of this book is to offer the public an introductory education on what a Demon is and the occurrence of Demonic Spirit attachment and possession that afflicts a large portion of humanity selectively. It is also an instructional manual on how to Repel forces of darkness as we learn to raise our vibrations in Light.

Note: In order to grasp the concepts discussed here book readers will benefit by being somewhat knowledgeable students of metaphysics. A glossary is included towards the end of the book to assist novices.

Table of Contents: **Page**

Note to reader: This material is intended as an informational guide. The remedies, approaches and techniques described herein are meant to supplement, and not to be a substitute for, professional medical/psychological care or treatment. They should not be used to treat a serious ailment without prior consultation with a qualified mental or physical health care professional.

Acknowledgments

I express gratitude for all of the spirit entities that attached to me throughout my life. They have enabled me to provide a fuller education to all for the betterment of human understanding and healing. Thanks to (birth attachment), Malchor, Palestinian warrior that confused my sexual identity, while gratefully, providing me with heightened feelings of testosterone when I was threatened by male abusiveness. Thank you to my great maternal grandmother with her five attachments that forced me to find forgiveness for my own childhood molestation.

My eternal gratitude to the Harrington family for a lifetime of loving support and to the Angels, Spirit Guides and Ascended Masters for exposing and fine tuning my education in the area of dark force manipulation. I feel the greatest appreciation for all of these Divine lighted ones (including humans) for backing me up and pressing me forward in order that I might prevail in bringing this darkness to light. And gratitude especially for my soul mate, Dorgeck, who coached me on these subjects and co-authored each book with mastery, loving generosity and wisdom. Now, we can make greater strides in healing our world one soul at a time.

*~ We dedicate this book to beloved
Idahohl-Adameus (Aka St Germain) ~*

Introduction

In this book we intend to shine greater light on the forces of darkness that have been trying to rule this planet to some degree for thousands of years. There are many experts in the Alternative News media expounding knowledgeably about these Dark Forces; their control and manipulations of governments and financial institutions. My personal commentary focuses only on the area of personal physical, mental and soul manipulation from a spiritual perspective.

I have become educated on the overall subject of planetary Dark Force control through the encouragement of my Angel and Spirit Guidance. It is our intent to expose only the *invisible* invasions and manipulations of the human mind, body and soul. I speak of the workings of darkness from the perspective of one who has overcome the many obstacles that the dark unseen forces have placed before me throughout my lifetime. My own personal experience and knowledge has been greatly expanded by the thousands of readers and clients I've interfaced with in my Mediumship practice that have been tormented with entity attachments, possessions and hauntings. This kind of activity by the Dark Forces causes a great portion of our population to be ineffective contributors to society, for much if not all their lives.

Demons are not a common topic of discussion except in the controversial 'conspiracy theory' sources that explore the Dark Forces surrounding the Illuminati. I believe the subject of Demonic influence within humanity needs to be included in the spiritual, psychological and healing forums of radio and TV talk shows and other public discussions where the physical and mental health professionals are likely to be present. The earth's population needs to be educated in this area of darkness so that the healers; physicians, psychotherapists, psychiatrists and alternative health practitioners (including priests) can expand awareness of what they are witnessing and diagnosing in patients. This is where extended healing work needs to be done that I, as a diagnostic and shamanic medium, am not qualified to do.

Demonic possession/attachment causes such severe trauma in many clients that they are literally unable to focus and work normally in life without professional assistance. As an empath, an emotional and physical 'sensitive', I have also experienced the effects of long-term cumulative trauma simply from working closely with Demonically possessed clients. For this reason, I only offer selective service of exorcism and ask many clients suffering from serious PTSD to seek out help from professional Spirit Releasement Therapists (SRT). I feel that even this may be a crapshoot for clients considering the lack of factual knowledge that exists in society on the subject of Demons. It is my hope that this material, developed through the teachings of God's Spiritual Hierarchy; the Ascended Masters and Angels, will help raise the awareness of medical and mental health professionals. These are the professional individuals that need education the most as they might otherwise continue to prescribe detrimental drugs and treatments for issues misdiagnosed as Bipolar, Borderline Personality Disorder, Dissociative Identity Disorder, Schizophrenia, Psychosis, etc.

CHAPTER ONE

Demon – What Are They - True or False?

If we are to understand a Demon we need to understand what and how their controlling forces manifest on the earth. We can look, if only briefly, to what is called the Illuminati; often touted as a 'conspiracy theory' concept. Many conspiracy theory groups exist to promote information exposing the dark forces that have oppressed humanity for millions of years.

My individual training is guided under the authority of Idahohl-Adameus-St. Germain, (Elohim Commander of Ascended Masters). From this point forward I will refer to Ascended Master Guides as AMG.

AMG's have confirmed that there are Fallen Elohim Angels with an agenda to overthrow the Light efforts of our Spiritual Hierarchy and keep humanity in the darkness as much as possible. The purpose of this is to serve the greed of those in power so they may grow richer, more self-indulgent and rule with ever greater power in darkness.

The Demon forces are behind those in the greatest power on earth. The AMG have guided me to understand that the governments and financial organizations in all of the major developed countries including the US and the Roman Catholic Church are affected by the influence of Demonic forces. I do not believe all of these leaders are evil. It is extremely likely however, that they have been afflicted with Demonic influences to some degree despite their individual intents, simply by holding positions of great power and influence.

It is not the author's purpose to expose specific details of the Illuminati leaders and organizations but only to include them in general terms in this discussion so that readers can explore further if desired. Information on the Illuminati may be found by typing the word into the Internet search engines. I was personally guided to pay attention to David Icke as a worthy introduction to the subject. Of course, this is an alternative news source and should be treated accordingly with our own common sense judgment and inner guidance. *WARNING: I would offer a **serious** caution for particularly sensitive people. You will *not* want to delve too deeply into this area of research.

The AMG guide me to understand that **in the beginning** of creation God/Goddess created lesser God's, called Elohim to help create the universe and to populate all of the planetary systems with life forms such as humans and animals. Some of the Elohim became very impressed with their own power and decided to see for themselves how powerful they could become. Of course, in order to glorify their own power they turned away from God and worked towards their own intent and purposes. This was their downfall. These Elohim fell from God's grace and became known as the "Fallen Angels" that humans refer to most often as Demons.

Important note: _Only a portion of the Elohim turned away from God._ Very many Elohim are working with the Divine Spiritual Hierarchy to restore light to the world and the universes!

~0~

AMG Othello has offered clarification on the issue of Demons.

Othello Speaks:

"You have learned that the Fallen Elohim were at the start of the **Demon inception**. It is their omnipresence and magical abilities that were distorted by their dark intent and this enabled them to be brilliantly evil once they turned.." (away from God). ".. and it was only their greed for power, to be omnipresent, to be the ONE with the power that they coveted from our Source/God and distorted it so greatly that they became very, very ugly. And it is a mystery to many how such genius can be within a Demon mind and ability. It is to know beloved that these are the Fallen Elohim Angels that have *become so very mighty and this is what gives them such genius of evil."*

Evolutionary Process of the Human Soul

> For the reader's understanding, it is necessary to make a distinction between the Elohim Creator Angels and Evolutionary Human Angels.
>
> The Evolution of the Human Soul described below does not include the subject of Fallen Elohim Angels.

To understand the nature of a human Angel it is helpful to begin with the human soul's evolutionary process as the AMG teachings explain. At our soul's inception we are each *incarnated to a material world, such as earth, to develop spiritually. At the end of our earthly life, we return to the Spirit Realms to continue our spiritual evolvement until we achieve an equivalent of Self Mastery (aka Ascended Master). Reaching Ascended Mastery may take hundreds or thousands of years or more. Christhood follows Ascended Mastery automatically and fairly quickly. When a human soul achieves Ascended Mastery/Christhood they are automatically assigned to the Angelhood Orders for training and eventual graduation as 1 of 9 types of Angels (accurately described by the Catholic Church doctrine). So, it is that Angels also began as humans in the spiritual evolutionary cycle. The possibility of a human Angel falling from grace is so extremely unlikely that it is not worth further discussion, according to the AMG.

<u>Levels of Evolutionary Attainment</u>

Evolution of the Human Soul

Spheres of Consciousness

▾

7-8th Spheres & above = Spiritual Hierarchy
7th Sphere - Elohim Creator Angels, Angelhood Order, Ascended Masters + Christ
6th Sphere - High vibration
5th Sphere - Medium-High vibration
4th Sphere - Medium vibration
3rd Sphere - Low to Medium vibration
2nd Sphere - Lower to Dark vibration
1st Sphere - Darkest and Demonic vibration

Throughout the remainder of this book the term Fallen Angels will refer to Elohim Angels only (not to spiritually evolved Human Angels).

*Note: It is incorrectly believed throughout much of society that many lifetimes are served through the reincarnation process in order to learn and evolve into Ascended Mastery. This popular (but false) belief is exposed in a new light in ***Reincarnation - The Four Factors - *** *Soul Freedom Vol 1* by the same authors Rise' Harrington & Bryan Jameison.

The Perspective of the Catholic Church

Concerning Demons

Q & A:

All references to the opinions of the Catholic Church are selectively paraphrased from Fr José Antonio Fortea's writings in his book titled *Interview with an Exorcist*. The Ascended Masters who guide me on the subject of Demons and the afterlife soul condition consider José Antonio Fortea's views on the subject of demons to accurately mirror the general opinion of the Catholic Church. It is myself with the AMG that offers a higher spiritual truth following each statement of the Catholic Church perspective.

What is a Demon?

Catholic Church: A Demon is a Fallen Angel that has been condemned for all of time, by God, to a mental, emotional and spiritual state of hell or purgatory.

Rise'/AMG: Condemnation is not of love and therefore is not in God's expression. God would not and has never condemned anything or anyone. God is all forgiving and allows all hearts to return to the path towards union with Him/Her whenever they choose to do so. When an Angel turns away from God's love/light they *unwittingly* close this door of light and love. This is the darkened Angels free will choice to cut themselves off from God and live in darkness! What may seem like condemnation is the karmic law consequence which will be settled in the souls' cycle of life.

Can a Demon cause a mental illness in a person?

<u>Catholic Church</u>: (In brief) "Yes."

<u>Rise'/AMG</u>: The Catholic Church and AMG agree that Demons can and do cause mental illness. Note: The following statements that I claim to be spiritual truth are from my own experience and schooling from the AMG teachings. Please pay attention to your own heart's resonance.

Demons can cause disturbance to the mental welfare of a human being through full possession, haunting or attachment.

The most predominant targets for Demon attachment (and possession) are those that are born into environments of ignorance and darkness. This is where ancestral influences are darkest. It has been passed down through the generations to favor oneself rather than one's child or grandchild by creating bargains with Satan in trade for descendent souls.

Full **Demon Possession** occurs only during the birth process through Demon attachment in the womb. These pre-birth possessions are effective attempts to prevent humans from growing into their full expression of being. A Demon possession causes a child to be born with many mental illnesses, most commonly: Autism, Asperger's and Downs Syndromes. It seems only Asperger's *might* be healed through exorcism if caught early enough in childhood. I have received confirming indication of this through only one client so far.

The healing of 14-year-old Mike S' Aspergers symptoms was not immediate but was witnessed by his family over the weeks and months following his exorcism.

From *Testimonial Page* of our website: http://guidelights.org Letters from Rhonda S (mother) and Mike S (son).

Following Demon Removal: Rhonda S.
November 4, 2013
Dear Rise'

Rebirth is precisely the word to describe Michael. Mike had been diagnosed with high functioning Asperger's by the age of 7. Until that time, we had no idea what was causing his emotional disturbances. Although he was a sweet child with an incredible sense of adult-like humor, he exhibited signs of extreme OCD / anxiety and had difficulty making and keeping friends. Mealtime was especially frustrating as Mike could not eat with our family or join the kids at school. He would sit at the far end of a dining table, away from breathing, coughing, talking....food untouched.

As Mike matured (13-14), he was better able to control his tantrums, but still had difficulty making and keeping friends. He began joining us at the dinner table and was no longer obsessed with germs, however, other symptoms began to appear. He would complain of headaches and sharp pains in his head. He had ongoing joint pain (all over his body, but primarily his lower back) and often displayed symptoms of appendicitis.

For 18 months, Mike was back and forth to the doctor. Extensive blood tests, CAT scans and an MRI ruled out all of the scary medical possibilities. At our last doctor visit, the doctor suggested that Mike might be exaggerating his pain, which made me feel both angry and hopeless. I could see the dark circles under his eyes and was watching him waste away. It became quite clear that whatever was wrong was not going to be "fixed" by a medical doctor.

One day, Mike produced a pencil drawing of the pain he was experiencing. It was a profile picture of himself with a demon-like creature attached to his back. The spiked tail of this creature was sticking into his lower back. About two weeks later, you fixed him. :-) *See Mike's drawing at the end of this article.

At first, we did not tell Mike about you, but his transformation was still astounding. Within a week, he said he had practically no pain at all. He was sleeping better, his ravenous appetite returned and so did his smile. Over the coming weeks the changes were incredible!! He began daily to express true heartfelt JOY! Smiling, singing, playing his guitar... almost immediately, his peers began to join him at lunchtime and ask him to "hang out". Within just a few weeks, he was invited to his first ever party and the friends keep on coming!

He is almost a different person; I know it's Mike, but it's not? Most signs of his Asperger's are completely gone. And while we are all enjoying Michael more than ever, it's not without a little bit of sadness on my part. I was mother to an angry, pained, suicidal, needy child that is no longer with us.   I know he's in a better place and I will always love him.

Mike says that he feels like completely different person (so much so, that he might like to change his name)! He explained that for most of his life, he was looking out of someone else's eyes and feeling emotionally numb.

Our appreciation of you is never-ending. We will

always be grateful to you for embracing your gift and sharing it with us. I believe that you literally saved my child's life! We have shared our story with many of our friends and family members and directed folks to your website and your book.
We thank God everyday for you, your gifts and your clarity!

Rhonda
St Louis, Mo 2013

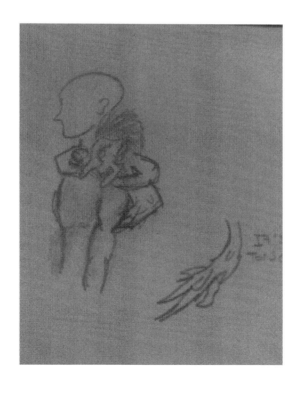

Hi, Rise! It's Michael.
I wanted to send this email to you personally because I wanted to say thank you for all the help you've done for me, my mother, my family, and for the advice you gave my teachers (They thank you personally). I feel more myself than I ever have in my 15 years of breathing, feeling, learning, and experiencing life. I have begun to understand my emotions more, people more, and that I cannot be a perfect person, but I can only be a good person with positive intentions. I've learned I am a human with a big role and I thank you for helping me realize that. I will treat life and people preciously with everything I've learned and put it towards changing the lives of everybody for the good everyone.

I wish the best for you and once again, thank you.
    ~Michael S~
St Louis, Mo 2014

----------------------------- * 0 * --------------------------

Demon Attachment can occur at any time in a person's life after birth.

Demonic attachment causes great traumatic disruption within a person's mind, body and spirit. This can cause mental disturbances such as Post Traumatic Stress Disorder (PTSD), sleeplessness, and Psychiatric diagnoses of Bipolar Disorder, Schizophrenia (seeing and hearing destructive visions and voices), Psychosis and suicidal depression. Demon attachments can also result in physical illnesses caused by extreme psychological stress.

What are the causes of Demon possession?

Catholic Church: The chief causes of possession are:

1 - Making a pact with the Devil.
2 - Taking part in esoteric or satanic cult rituals.
3 - Offering one's child to Satan.
4 - Being the victim of a spell.

AMG' response/teaching:

1 - Pact with the Devil
Anyone that invites darkness into their life gives their power away to or unites it with evil may unconsciously invite invasion of a Demon attachment.

People in a dark frame of mind might be more likely to pray to dark powers like Satan or Devil figures rather than Light such as Angels or God/Goddess. I imagine this to be a circumstance where children are raised with a serious level of neglect physically and/or emotionally by one or both of their parents. Children of abuse and neglect are likely to be left to flounder in darkness. Focusing on darkness and figures of darkness will most certainly draw Demons into one's own private mental and physical domain.

I believe such was the case with the Parkland, Florida high school killings of over 15 students by a 19-year-old (2018). Before that, the gentleman massacring almost 60 people in Las Vegas (2017). Naturally mentally disturbed human beings do not possess a superhuman desire to massacre human beings to this extent. But Demonic forces do and will cajole, talk to and twist the human brain to configure and execute these mass murders. They receive superhuman evil strength and energy to conduct these most horrendous executions. That is why these events are thought of as *inhumane* acts.

Thankfully not all humans that attract Demons through pacts with Satan will become mass murderers.

2 - Practicing Dark Magic or Satanic Rituals

If we dabble in the esoteric or spiritual realms without protection and a stated intention to speak and interface only with Divine Beings of Light, we are exposing ourselves to serious danger. We might accidentally (or intentionally) invite creepy energies to join us or cause ourselves to be susceptible to hauntings and dark soul entity and Demon attacks.

I have had various clients who worked with some lesser degree of the dark side's offerings. Some just dabble in the dark perhaps through dark magic and rituals. *Those that suffer the consequences of dabbling are easier to help because they are more likely to attract only Demon hauntings instead of an attachment. Haunting means a Demon shadows the human continually attempting to attach but is unable to. Depending on the clients focus and intent when they ask for help from a medium, they may be able to help themselves without exorcism by simply raising their vibrations and determinedly focusing devotionally on the light. This is where I step in to practice light work counseling. In this case they can often change their attraction/haunting by changing their focus to light/love and working very diligently to raise their vibration. Demons are REPELLED by LIGHT and LOVE!*

Light/love work mental reprogramming is not easy. It takes constant vigilance inwardly with the management of one's thoughts and focus/imaginings. But, with determination, it is possible, and it works very effectively for self-help healing! There is much more to come on this subject.

3 - **Pledging Child or Grandchild to Satan -** **(Ancestral Curses)**

The AMG agrees that offering one's descendent child to Satan will cause the child to be Demon Possessed if it is still in the womb. If the child is already born when the offering to Satan is made the child will only receive a Demon Attachment which is also a terrible affliction.

This is very much the same as the first circumstance of making a pact with the devil. Bargaining with the devil, whether or not there is a descendent child, results in the same consequence. In the first circumstance only the bargainer receives a Demon haunting or attachment. When bargaining for trade with a descendent soul, the ancestor and offspring both receive Demon afflictions.

4 - **Victim of spell**
A dark witch can summon a Demon but cannot force the possession of a soul whose belief system and personal light vibration does not allow for this. This is based on the universal Law of Attraction (LOA) which runs the universe.

There are other systems of curses and spells used by dark forces through Alien technologies aligned with Demon Satanic forces. The subject will be covered in our section titled **IMPLANTS.** For further information on **Implants** and **Black Magic Curses** (Witchcraft Spells) see our book:

Entity Attachment Removal - Self-Help Procedure - The ABC of Releasing Spirit Attachments for Do It Yourselfers -Soul Freedom Series Vol 3

Symptoms of Demon Attachment

(Aka Possession)

As we've already presented, full Demon possessions only happen in pre-birth and causes serious mental illness. To society this just looks like a serious mental illness.

Demon's that *attach* post birth are able to take control of the human physical and mental faculties only *intermittently* and the rest of the time the human child or adult may be thought of as normal or sane. They will not, however, *feel good* to a sensitive person. Here are some symptoms that might be experienced by someone who has a Demon attachment.

Anorexia
Feelings of darkness, misery, desolation, etc.
Feeling like being a witness to your life.
Long-term depression and suicidal thoughts.
Losing blocks of present time awareness and memory.
Sexual interference and/or attack to groin area.
Self-mutilation
Seeing freakish or evil visions.
Strange voices speaking to you abusively; lying and threatening.
* Bites and scratches from an unseen source.

* Physical manipulation of limbs – loss of mobility control.
* Speaking foreign languages that have not been studied.
* Telekinesis - **Violent** telekinetic movement and breakage of objects.
* **Violence** against animals and humans.

Note: Some of these symptoms are not necessarily specific to Demon Attachment and might also be common to dark soul entity attachments and hauntings. We have used an *asterisk to mark those that are usually specific to symptoms of *Demon Attachments.

**Note: Lost souls may also cause violent acts against animals and humans *only if* several of them join forces with the common intent to do harm. This would be a group act of violence. A lost soul acting on its own cannot summon enough energy to cause an act of violence against animals or humans.

What a Demon Is Not

A Demon can shape shift into seeming lovely energy beings such as fairies, beautiful animals, popular figures such as famous entertainers and movie stars in attempts to trap humans. However, no matter how **beautiful** a Demon may appear it will always *feel* dark, untrustworthy and ugly. We should always follow our instinctive and intuitive feelings if there is any question about the authenticity of what is occurring in our waking or dreaming awareness.

Trust beautiful apparitions *only* when they _feel_ truly beautiful.

CHAPTER TWO

Possession, Haunting and Attachment

Once an Elohim Angel falls from grace, he/she is drawn vibrationally by the Law of Attraction (LOA) from the heavenly realms down to the darkest sphere of the Spirit Realms. They now exist as Demon beings and reside in what is frequently called the underworld.

Universal Law prevents a Demon who is operating in the Spirit Realms from intruding itself onto the earth plane. Dark interference from the Spirit Realms can only be executed from the *astral* plane. So, How do demons attack, attach to and possess humans? A workaround was developed. The Demon forces devised a tactic to manipulate humans through the **astral realms**.

The astral realm is an atmospheric environment of spirit surrounding the earth and the universe. It is a field of travel between spheres (levels) of consciousness. The astral realm is also used to temporarily house the souls that become lost or stuck in the death transition between earth and the Spirit Realms.

Souls that become lost are radiating at vibrations of light, dark and varying shades in between. The newly deceased lost souls are in the most disorientation and turmoil. It is these that lash out and attract the attention of the demonic ones. It is only the darkest lost souls in the astral realms that can and will attack human souls on the earth (3rd dimension). Therefore, it is these dark lost souls housed in the astral realm *(4th dimension) that are captured by Demons and used to access the humans on earth for Demonic manipulation.

*Many readers consider the astral realm to be a fourth dimensional environment. It is only for the sake of common understanding that I mention it here as fourth dimensional.

In the Realms of Spirit there are many Spheres of Consciousness coexisting at different vibratory rates. Mankind refers to the varying vibrations on earth in terms of dimensions but in spirit the vibratory rate refers to spheres of consciousness as we list here. There are many additional higher spheres of consciousness than we list in our presentation. This is an Ascended Master teaching, as I understand it. *Note.

7-8th Spheres & above = Spiritual Hierarchy
7th Sphere - Elohim Creator Angels, Angelhood Order, Ascended Masters + Christ
6th Sphere - High vibration
5th Sphere - Medium-High vibration
4th Sphere - Medium vibration
3rd Sphere - Low to Medium vibration
2nd Sphere - Lower to Dark vibration
1st Sphere - Darkest and Demonic vibration

*Note Ref: AJ Miller DivineTruth.com Playlist "Through The Mists"

We might ask. How do these Fallen Angel/Demons take up residency on earth to negatively affect humanity?

The Demons use the astral field to reach through the atmosphere of lost souls in order to enlist the darkest ones. The Law of Attraction (LOA) causes the darkest souls to gravitate to demon forces quite naturally. Demons then attach the dark souls to the Demon's Caterpillar-like body. These souls are now willing Demon **Slaves** in service to the Demon. The caterpillar is used as an analogy for the Demons energy body to demonstrate the different body compartments holding individual slaves. The Demon can trap and attach up to eight dark souls to complete its full assembly. The head/brain is the originating Demon and the compartments in the body are the attached dark entity slaves. The attached slaves enable the Demon to <u>contain sufficient humanness to take up residency on the earth</u>.

Demons slaves have pledged allegiance to the parent Elohim demon before becoming attached to the parent demon. A truer analogy would be to see these slaves tethered to the parent like a tetherball to a steel post in a children's playground.

A Demon Slave will often hover over a human target and wait for a weakened moment to attach to the body. This is a period of haunting that can proceed attachment. A person that is experiencing a Demon haunting with attachment attempts often feels haunted by many entities because of all the demon brethren slaves that are attached to the parent Demon.

Once the Demon slave attaches it is now in coexisting control of this human for its lifetime unless there is; 1) intervention by an exorcist/spiritual healer or, 2) the human evolves to a high spiritual radiation of light that repels the Demon slave into dormancy. In the second case the human has taken full control of its own souls free will choice and returned to full embodiment of light. Such was my case as described below.

Explanation of Demon Slaves:

As explained previously, the astral realm that houses the lost soul population is universal and therefore includes human and alien souls that are lost. Demons are intergalactic beings and possess dark lost souls from all races in the universe. Therefore, a human might experience an Alien Demon or Human Demon. So far, in the work I have done with clients the impact of alien versus human Demon is not an important distinction beyond general interest.

The night before I removed my own alien demon many years ago, I saw the image of a two headed being exacerbated by a wobbling affect. This image was instrumental only in giving me the clue I needed to determine it was an alien soul. Because I had gained enough light radiation within me the demon effects had already been muted (become dormant). It was not a demon that I removed but a dormant demon slave attachment.

Do not underestimate the demonic power of the darkest soul when considering that it is only a human or alien soul. As a willing slave it has pledged allegiance to the Fallen Angel Demon and possesses all of its abilities and powers of evil genius.

What is the goal of Demonic Attachment and Possession?

To enable the darkest agenda in creation. To rule all planetary resources and all souls prominent in forces of responsibility in order to *extinguish* the light.

CHAPTER THREE

Repelling Demons and Dark Forces

Raising Our Vibrations

In the most ideal circumstance, we have all been raised by human adults that were people with very good values and ethics. If that were the case, then there wouldn't a reason to read this book or a need to uncover and understand the opposite side of the coin.

There are an endless number of valuable reasons to justify being a beautiful soul on the earth with wonderful ethics and values. In this book we will focus mainly on what is necessary to prohibit dark forces from interfering and intruding upon our souls and our lives.

This discussion is based on the values of good and evil and the Law of Attraction (LOA) which is the universal law created to attract to us that which we radiate outwardly.

LOA means that positive or negative thoughts bring positive or negative experiences into a person's life. Positive = Good or high vibration. Negative = Bad or low vibration.

What makes this particularly difficult to present is that the most purely vibrating child or adult will experience demonic assault caused by ancestral curse through no fault of their own. *However*, the fact that the child or adult is high in vibration makes it easier for them and their support systems to repel the demon into dormancy.

This means that when we have a demon attached to our soul that it may be suspended by continual light infusion which causes it to be dormant within us. It becomes inactive through the consistent and regular infusion of light. I can speak of this with some authority because I had one within me that I carried for 30 years. I had assumed that it was a very dark being that I had grown out of or that had left me after so long until I started to learn about dark forces, demonic possessions and entity attachments. Reference the works of William J. Baldwin, Ph.D. *Healing Lost Souls* and Dr. Edith Fiore *The Unquiet Dead.*

I discovered using self-help methods while trying to extinguish the darkness within me, for so much of my life, how to literally Repel Darkness. These included an entity birth attachment, trauma attachments and at age 21 an ancestral curse of demon attachment. This journey resulted in the publishing of my first book *Guide Lights* which documented the path that I learned to work within to become illuminated. This enabled me to eliminate all of the soul intrusions including the demon attachment. Really consistent and continual carriage of light essentially vibrated them out of existence in my life! Of course, each had to be individually removed as well but causing their dormancy prior to removal eased the path for me *enormously*. Ref: *Entity Attachment Removal - Self-Help Procedure - The ABC of Releasing Spirit Attachments for Do It Yourselfers -Soul Freedom Series Vol 3.*

*It is important to note here that repelling darkness or dark entities does not free our souls to be as free in divine light as God intended. These entities still have to be removed by ourselves, a practiced medium or (SRT) Spirit Release Therapist for us to achieve true soul freedom.

The following is an excerpted chapter of masterful lessons from **Guide Lights - Attune to Your Angels and Spirit Guides** adapted for inclusion in this book. These are necessary to learn in order to repel attacking darkness through our love and light and are a prerequisite to repel the darkness that exists within our own souls. Once we hold sufficient light over the dormant demonic entities an expert Shaman, Priest or Healer is enabled to permanently remove or exorcise a Demon from our soul. Although a demon may want to return to the human, they are no longer able to for the light radiation is too great. **Radiant light/love carriage is the only shield that enables the permanency of demon exorcism**.

*Excerpt: from **Guide Lights Attune - to Your Angels and Spirit Guides** Chapter 4:*

Raise Your Light Level ~ Get in the Flow

Vibration is the emanation of consciousness (as energy) in varying degrees of light or dark. How we think, eat and behave is impressed upon the personal energy that we radiate. If we were measured, as an average, most of us would range in vibration between varying shades of grayish colors – not light or dark, but somewhere in between.

Raising the vibrations of our physical, mental and emotional self is necessary to achieve and maintain a strong connection to Divine Spirit. When our vibrations are raised, we emanate lighter energy, and the gap between physical and spiritual dimensions is lessened. This makes our communications with the higher realms much easier and the depth of our experiences richer.

It is necessary to practice a lifestyle of light and positive attitude in order to grow spiritually in our relationship with God's messengers. Development of this lifestyle is accomplished in the same way we learn any other skill or discipline. There are ups, downs, and periods of progress in between. No matter how hard we study, we will sometimes fail tests, feel down in the dumps, and even lose faith once in a while.

As we experience the ups and downs of the spiritual initiate we can, at times, feel lost and disconnected. Our prayers seem to go out into an empty void. When we're in a negative or depressed place mentally and emotionally, our communications are actually dimmed. The heaviness of our vibrations weakens our connection to Spirit and disables us from being able to sense the loving attention of our Angels and Spirit Guides. We are also prevented from receiving or recognizing the answers from Spirit to our requests for guidance. A barrier has been erected between realms to protect the light from our darkness. <u>We are the unwitting creators of this barrier.</u>

When we are vibrating at a high frequency, we feel uplifted, at peace and inspired. We've all experienced this feeling at times in our lives when we've been moved by a beautiful piece of music, an inspiring film or a new romantic love. These times of upliftment and soaring of the heart are usually short-lived, but at least for moments they inspire feelings of peace, love and happiness that fuel our souls. We are temporarily awakened to the underlying and all-pervasive presence of God's loving genius in the world.

~ o ~

In the beginning we were formed into being from the light of our Creator. Over time we became lost to the light, and we have lived through the ages in semi-darkness. There are many theories about how and why we lost the connection to our light heritage. At this point we don't need to explore the reasons we became disconnected, but we do need to reawaken to the light within us so that it can once again illuminate our lives!

So, how do we reclaim our light? We can learn to create a framework of intention that sets us up to experience moments of magic and wonder in our lives much more frequently. This concept embraces the principle of positive thinking at its very best. The intent is to create feelings of peace, love and joy without waiting for life to bless us with seemingly random experiences of divine inspiration. We can create these desired feelings by reprogramming our thoughts and choosing a lifestyle dedicated to living in the light.

Here is an example of positive intention and mindset:

~I intend to think positively – *no matter what.*
~I look to see the positive in all things. If I am unable to see it now, I have faith that I'll eventually

see the aspects of good in all my experiences. Perhaps there's a lesson to be learned.

~I am willing to be open, receptive, and tolerant of others. I release all criticism and judgment. There is something lovable in *everyone*.

~I practice an attitude of patience and forgiveness.

~I do not let fearful thinking rule any of my moments. I place my fears in God's hands and release them for the highest outcome to unfold.

~ Faith, trust and hope are my guiding forces - I have faith in the processes of life.

~I am grateful for all the blessings in my life. I understand that a focus of gratitude creates a continued abundance of blessings in every aspect of my life.

~I let love be my guiding force always including times of trouble and uncertainty.

*Tag this page with a marker so you can return frequently for pattern changing reminders!

~ o ~

As we practice positive thinking and loving behaviors, we begin to experience the flow. This is the force of God's spirit flowing through all of life on a much higher vibrational scale than we're used to living in. The flow is divine love-light in motion, moving forward, intertwining all of us in the one spiritual flow, arranging divine expression for the highest good of all.

The flow is a very natural part of life and is very accessible to all of us. Sometimes the flow just happens to us like a magically timed interlude in our life plan. When we're very spiritually evolved and/or truly love our work, we're in the flow quite naturally much of the time. Love is the very essence of light, and when we embrace it as our mode of operation Spirit draws all of the things we need into our lives like a magnet.

For those still floundering in the semi-darkness, these interludes of flow seldom occur. Most of the time, we have to make a clear choice to practice being in the light to get ourselves into the flow. Practicing reprograms our thinking into new, more positive ways of being.

With practice we become more and more accustomed to being in a lighter space with extended periods of inner peace and feelings of contentment. The greater the determination in our practice, the easier it gets.

Self-Mastery ~ God's Toilet

Walking this path consciously is making the choice to take responsibility for Mastery of self in creation of our lives and futures. Choosing to manage the thoughts I entertain in my mind enables me to be a person of Self-Mastery.

It is not easy. Many of us have been subjected to negativity and difficult circumstance for much, if not, all of our lives. If it has been constant, by the time we're young adults it's very ingrained in us. We continue to carry the worst of our families and society in our consciousness, the brain storing the programs and the patterns that have been running repetitive tapes within us all our lives. Self-pity, fear, old stories, self-criticism, revenge, curses, hate, old patterns, doubt, judgment etc.

Some may say, "Well, I can't help what goes through my mind!"

Who can? Do you think your creator God put these programs and patterns into place? Certainly not. Your life experience has programmed your subconscious mind through your circumstance and your reaction to it. You have used your own God-given free will choice to accept, reject, fear, retaliate, become victimized, run away from etc.

This happened to me repetitively. Bummer. He says, she says. It happens. They always do. I can't stop it. I can't help it. What the heck am I supposed to do about it?

Release it down God's Divine Receptacle and flush it.

God will take your mental trash and recycle it into Divine Light.

Recognize - Flush - Affirm

So, once you recognize a negative thought pattern, imagine the divine toilet in front of you whether you are sitting, standing or walking. Imagine the thought stream flushing down the divine white, cosmic toilet. And then, replace the negative thought with an affirmative. *I forgive them, I will learn the positive lesson from that. I decide to be positive this day no matter what. All negative things have a positive truth inside. Truth can be found in every circumstance. God leads me forward into light. It is always my choice what I choose to think and feel!*

Remember the little engine that could? *I think love, I think light,* **I think I can** *choose only love and light!* I think I can, I think I can, I think I can achieve self-mastery over darkness!

Do this over and over again. Think, release, flush and then affirm a positive replacement. I still do this throughout my days when necessary. **It is my choice until I leave this earth; to purify my mind, to love myself for taking command and to be at peace.**

This is how we eventually reach a high vibrational light and love that enables us to talk to Angels as God's messengers. We practice over and over again, day after day after year after decade so that our vibrations are so high and loving that negativity and darkness can hardly reach us any longer. Only for moments at a time as we emotionally struggle with the downsides of life with loved ones and other earthly relations. Then we pick ourselves up and immediately get back on track affirming all things of positivity, light and love again.

It's *not* easy - but it is simple!

By practicing the simple processes designed to raise our vibrations, we are naturally uplifted into the light. Embodied within the emanation of light is the *flow*. When we're walking, talking and *being* the light, all our senses are open and flowing, transmitting and receiving, in the *flow*. This is when we experience miracles of divine synchronicity, those marvelous coincidences, lucky events, and momentous inspirations.

When we're in the *flow* we move toward the life of our greatest potential and spontaneously express our unique gifts fully attuned to the spirit in all things. We're fully living in the present moment. We are not carrying the past or future with us; we are simply in the NOW.

We've all heard the words from the Book of Proverbs, "as a man thinketh in his heart, so he is." Be on guard - your own affirmations and beliefs are creating your future! Will it be positive or negative, light or dark? It's up to you.

Does this sound overly simplified? It truly is that simple. No one else has the power to make you think a single thought. You are the sole commander of your mind and the company you keep within it. It is always your choice.

I am not suggesting that acquiring the self-discipline needed to change your mindset from negative to positive is easy. It is extraordinarily difficult for so many of us – but it is simple! *You have the opportunity to take back your power NOW.*

Regardless of new positive intentions, negative thoughts *will* continue to pass through our minds now and then. They will only get us into trouble when we choose to entertain them and build on them. Negative thinking is learned behavior. The behavioral role models provided by our family and society have ingrained in us repetitive patterns of negative thinking. After twenty, thirty, or forty years of living with negative thought patterns it *seems* almost impossible to break them.

I am still susceptible to negative thought infiltrations and have to reverse them. Something in life will trigger a negative reaction in me and I'll immediately revisit old critical thought patterns. But now, I only allow myself to entertain these thoughts long enough to recognize them. I then create a reverse positive affirmation to neutralize and release (flush) the negative thought. The point is that I refuse to entertain negative or unhappy thoughts and immediately focus my attention on something neutral or positive. And since we're being honest here, I have to admit that I am not "in the flow" as often as I'd like to be as I write this book.

Sometimes being "in the flow" simply means being in non-resistance while dealing with challenging circumstances.

It's all about choice. No one has the power to make us think or feel anything. It's always our choice. We can choose to release a negative thought impulse or reaction at any moment, no matter what situation we're in. We are ultimately either in control of our thoughts or out of control in every moment, every day of our lives. Let's Fake It until we Make It!

Our thoughts cause us to feel emotion. Thoughts such as "I hate this, I resent that, I am always so broke" etc., stir up negative feelings within us. Negative emotions lower our vibration rate so that we become physically denser. Emotions like irritation, anger, hate, resentment and fear trigger physical symptoms within our bodies. We may experience a headache, nervousness, asthma, stomachache or high blood pressure. These are only a few of the short-term symptoms negative thinking may cause. Longer-term negative thinking can create much more serious physical implications.

The good news is that the practice of positive thinking fueled by positive emotion has an immediate short-term remedying effect. It changes the energy we are expressing and the way we feel emotionally and physically in the present moment. It can relax us, relieve headache, restore normal breathing and lower blood pressure instantly.

Long-term changes are achieved with continued practice. In the example of the "just my luck" person, a positive counter-affirmation repeated often enough will change the person's subconscious belief that he or she is unlucky. Example; "I am a worthy and valuable person. I allow my abundance to grow every day in every way". This states a positive intent to alter and eventually change a negative belief. Just make sure that whatever affirmation you choose to counteract a negative belief or thought pattern is reasonable. To be effective, it needs to be something *you* can reasonably believe. Choosing to counter a thought of "I am broke" with "I am rich!" is not an effective approach. "I have everything I need in life as I need it" is a more reasonable affirmation for your conscious and subconscious mind to accept in the beginning. You can improve on the scope of your affirmations as you progress. Ask the Angels to help you create the affirmations that will work best for you – and ask for assistance in remembering to use them! Affirmations take practice and determination, but they *absolutely* do work!

The single most important ingredient to making affirmations effective is *feeling*. Play, have fun. Act it out emotionally – feeling your desired

outcome is the key to successful conscious and subconscious programming and absolutely creates your future. *Feel* successful, *feel* powerful and *feel* abundant. F*eel* fortunate, loving and loved. You truly are these things when you reprogram your brain *(change your beliefs)* and *allow* yourself to be made anew.

Beginners on this path may find the reorientation to light-focused living quite a challenge. It takes determination and continual practice to maintain a light body, mind and spirit, especially in today's often chaotic world. It's okay to slip up. Just pick yourself up and get back on track. Do not chastise yourself for reverting to negative thought programs. If you slip up a hundred times in one day, congratulate yourself for paying attention and take corrective action 100 times. Pat yourself on the back for doing something positive to take command of your thoughts. Mental activity (thinking) is energy utilized. If we use our minds negatively, we actually *lose* energy. Positive thought is positive energy; it *energizes* us.

The more we practice light techniques and positive thinking, the longer we will be able to sustain light vibrations and feelings of inner peace. We lessen the gap between the higher and lower realms by lifting ourselves vibrationally to be more attuned with our Angels and Spirit Guides. As we learn to raise our light level, spirit guidance is more easily able to meet us halfway to assure clear connection between realms.

Another benefit to raising our light vibrations is the expanded consciousness that results over time. The intuitive or psychic gifts you already have will be magnified, and other skills will be developed quite naturally. When I first began light practices, I saw pale swirling colors and vague shapes in my inner vision. A couple of years later as my light quotient grew my intuitive gifts developed. I began to see with my inner vision the full shimmering light image of my Spirit Guide's face and sparkling eyes.

Light Techniques

How to Raise Your Own Frequency and the Vibration of Your Space.

All of the following methods provide an upliftment of the heart, mind and spirit, which in turn raises the light vibration of our physical bodies. These techniques have an immediate effect and can be sustained over time only if we continue to practice and renew them.

Establish a routine, if you can, for spiritual sessions. Select a space in your home or other place of choice where you are comfortable and have privacy. This can be inside or in nature. Perform all of your spiritual practices on a regular basis in this spot to begin with and make it your own sacred space. Setting up a special or sacred space is a good way to set the mood for spiritual sessions. Cleaning and uncluttering our meditative space and home is an important way to raise the vibrations of the environment and lighten the flow of energy around us.

Choose ideas from the following list to establish your special space and adapt your own ideas or preferences.

~Create an altar of your most precious things; crystals, Angels, figurines, herbs, incense.
Anything that makes you feel inspired, special, close to God and the Angels will greatly enhance your experience of upliftment and communion with Spirit.
~Light candles and incense.
~Burn white sage for the purification of energy surrounding your space.
~Listen to beautiful, soothing and relaxing music.
~Create your own sacred ritual of readiness for meeting with spirit for meditation or prayer.
~Think loving thoughts or repeat love affirmations with feeling.

As we focus on loving thoughts while really feeling the meaning of the words, we are uplifted spiritually. When I initially became dedicated to spiritual practice I meditated daily for long periods of time. In meditation I often repeated these words from the Beatles song: "All you need is love - love, love, love..." over and over again. I focused on feeling love to lift myself higher and to sustain this level long enough to achieve communion with the higher realms. Do whatever it takes, even if you feel silly. You have no witness except the loving beings of guidance you are reaching for. Your Angels and guides are cheering your every effort and sending waves of love to assist you.

~Read spiritual, religious or other uplifting books regularly. When you're down in the dumps, pick up your reading material for inspiration. Have a book of this sort in progress at all times or keep your favorite on hand to reread when needed.

~Listen to spiritually oriented teachings or audio books while you get ready in the morning, as you drive to work, or as you wind down in the evening.

~Spend quality time communing with nature.

~Keep a tall glass of water nearby at all times as a conductor of Spirit. Water accommodates spiritual communications as it magnifies the intuitive impressions we receive from Spirit.

Breathing Exercises

Breathing exercises are key to raising our vibrations and aligning our physical and spiritual bodies as one. As we breathe in deeply while simultaneously slowing our thoughts, we are going within ourselves, deep within to the core self, the quiet simplicity of being. The simple exercise described here is widely used and highly recommended by Spirit. Follow these instructions only to the extent that you can do them *comfortably*. <u>Do not strain yourself in any way</u>.

Sit in an upright position in loose comfortable clothing.

Make a conscious effort to inflate your abdomen as you breathe in. This will maximize the benefit of each breath.

Breathe deeply in through your nose to an approximate count of four and hold the breath for a count of four. Exhale fully through the mouth until the abdomen is empty (approximate count of six to eight).

Repeat this breath three times:

Inhale deeply through nose (**4** count)
Hold   (**4** count)
Exhale completely through mouth (**6-8** count)

You should feel slightly exhilarated by this exercise and experience an increased sense of calm. Use this breathing technique prior to meditation, channeling, performing healing and all other spiritually focused exercises.

~ o ~

Visualization is our most powerful tool of creation when accompanied by emotion.
If visualization is difficult for you, like color, imagine something like an object or scene very familiar to you. Try imagining a wedding band for the gold color and a rose as pink. For silver you might imagine the tinsel on a Christmas tree and for white a snowy landscape.

Each of the following visualization exercises will serve to raise your vibrations: *(Caution: doing these exercises at night may cause sleeplessness)*

White Light Technique (Adapted from – Edith Fiore)

Excerpt from "The Unquiet Dead"

"Imagine that you have a miniature sun, just like the sun in our solar system deep in your solar plexus. This sun is radiating through every atom and cell of your being. It fills you with light to the tips of your

fingers, the top of your head, and the soles of your feet. It shines through you and beyond you an arm's-length in every direction – above your head, below your feet, out to the sides, creating an aura – a brilliant, dazzling, radiant White Light that completely surrounds and protects you from any negativity or harm." End Excerpt.

The reason this exercise is so effective is that we are imagining the truth of God's living light inside of our bodies. I recommend the heart to be the center of this exercise as this is where our God spark exists but either the solar plexus or the heart chakra will be effective. As we fill up our bodies with this brilliant sparkling LIVING White Light you will feel God's presence within you!

~ o ~

~Visualize your aura expanding and becoming a brilliant pink, white or gold. Let yourself expand and become brilliant, radiating your light in an expanded circle around you. Sit quietly for some moments basking in your own new light filled aura.

~Visualize yourself taking a shower in white, silver or gold light rays pouring down from the heavens, washing over you. Imagine you *feel* the sweet, subtle rush of light penetrating every cell of your body, *infusing you with light. Feel yourself becoming* *lightened.* Bask in this light often; let yourself revel in the delightful radiance. ***(I highly recommend this method for immediate upliftment and rejuvenation.)

~Fill your workplace with the light of your choice to set a lighter tone. If you're having some difficulty at work, pink light will help to create a love vibration in the environment. Visualize pink light filling your workplace prior to going to work. The Angels will be happy to help you with this also; just ask for their assistance. This not only helps you but also benefits everyone in your workplace.

You can also project light to a future event that you plan to attend, or to any place you feel needs to be uplifted by light. I use this technique when venturing into a place I haven't visited before or a place I feel nervous about going to. The light then becomes the prevailing presence. When I arrive in an environment that I've treated with light beforehand, I feel comfortable as soon as I get there. Light is the substance of God's love. When used with high intent, it works wonders to create harmony and the highest outcome for every occasion.

Don't be concerned if you have difficulty visualizing colors or other images. When I began learning visualization techniques, I was unable to see the image I was trying to create. Instead, I *pretended* I could see the image. With practice this pretend imaging began to produce results. I began to see the image through my feeling senses and inner vision. Through feeling/sensing/seeing the color, I experience it fully in the way that is natural to me. My means of doing this may be very different from others. God has created each of us uniquely. Concentrate on the way that comes naturally to you instead of trying to match someone else's intuitive skills and abilities. In the event you can't visualize, simply pretend. It works!

Does it seem like we're just psyching ourselves out when we practice these kinds of ritualistic and imaginary exercises? *That is exactly what we're doing!* The practice of <u>imagining with feeling</u> creates a new reality of experience for us by convincing our subconscious minds that what we imagine is real. I believe this is how God created the world; through enormous loving emotion imagining the universe and humanity into being. Creating us in his/her image, giving each of us the same qualities of imagination and emotion to co-create our lives with love, peace, joy, and abundance.

I encourage you to practice these exercises daily or as often as you can. The practice of imagining ourselves as light stirs the soul memory of our divine nature. **Over time we begin to have glimpses of** who we really are; the spiritual/physical *personification of God's love expressed.*

~ o ~

CHAPTER FOUR

Emergence of Darkness in Times of Armageddon - Light Portals - Earth Illumination

Dorgeck Speaks:

"It is necessary to educate the public in this area of Armageddon as well. So, we do so with great hope and faith in the future from a perspective of those who have the light of knowing that the light will always ultimately overcome. So, it is not a warning so much as it is for comforting that we prepare and write about the light, about love; this is what saves the world, what saves humanity, what saves our universe, indeed!"

"We would say, that as we begin this day, we can overcome all evil and all darkness. We overcome all sediment of dirt, slime and grime and all such things of evil and dark intent as we discern for ourselves our own Sparks of Light that we grow within ourselves to become the Lighted Ones that are the ones of the greatest light to be grown and to expand in all others to exponentially create enormous flames of Glory Light, indeed!"

~ o ~

As we've learned, the first dark, evil intent was created through an Elohim Creator Angel using his/her free will choice to turn away from God to use power with their own evil intent. This is when the concept of Armageddon was also necessarily conceived. We need to see this as the beginning of the New Times; life renewed in love, not the end of all time.

"If we can imagine our lives for the moment to be of pure light and love in all of our moments, with freedom to express our individual natures and love in all regards in every moment of our lives then we can all be free for eternity, indeed."

We, in alignment with the Spiritual Hierarchy can help to create this by volunteering to be human Earth Anchors.

Light Portal - Earth Illumination

The Spiritual Hierarchy, also known as the White Brotherhood/Sisterhood, invite all of us to become Light Workers and **earth anchors** to help them spread Gods light to the earth and all of humanity.

This ceremony can be conducted in your home, on your balcony, backyard or anywhere on earth that feels comfortable to you. Claim silently or aloud, "I volunteer myself to the Divine orders of light and love as an earth anchor to be used by the Spiritual Hierarchy to lift the vibrations of the earth."

"I ask the spiritual hierarchy to help me bring God's WHITE LIGHT into the portal of my home to illuminate and heal the earth, all living creatures and souls upon the earth." Envision this as you can and feel it surrounding you as it flows through your space and body into the earth.

(I envision a portal to be a big funnel shaped opening between the realms of Spirit and Earth).

I allow this light to flow down from heaven through me and my home to move swiftly to the core center of the earth. The light now saturates the center of the earth and rises throughout illuminating the entire surface and consciousness of all living things and souls upon the earth for the highest good of all. This can be done as frequently or as seldom as you prefer. God's Spiritual Hierarchy requests that we contribute to the earth's light daily. In this, we are focused on illuminating the earth and mankind with God's truth of Love, Light and Peace for the highest good of all!

~ o ~

Dorgeck Speaks:

"So, we have begun with the news that the world is not coming to an end. It only seems so at times as the foretelling has overshadowed the earth for some

long time. Especially in world religions and biblical texts that encourage this thinking to some extent. We have others around the world who have derived slightly different interpretations of these notions and have put out other scare tactics into our societies through the grapevines of fear and discouragement of all kinds.

So, we may determine for ourselves as we move forward what is true and what is not.

And it is only the embrace of light and truth for ourselves as we pay attention to the God forces of our spirit realm; of Angels and Masters that we may embrace the truth. It is only these who speak for our God/Goddess who want so graciously to invite us home to the world of truth and brilliance of light that enlivens our hearts and souls for all of time forever and ever more. Indeed, it is so.

Let not our history remind us of the evils that are upon the earth, the Hitler's and such. Let us look forward to the new dawn that is breaking around the universe now as the light forces grow so strong that we cannot resist any longer, recognizing the embrace of our God in every bird, tree and breeze, indeed? So be it! We accept our grace as it enfolds us beloveds. The brilliance of our God on earth. So be it!"

EPILOGUE

Final words from Idahohl-Adameus (St. Germain):

"We would comment also that we need all to understand the purpose of this book is only to overwhelm with light, not to kill a single thing or to eliminate a single soul. It is only to eliminate dark power and make it very, very difficult to extinguish light, to overwhelm the light. The dark will be much excluded for eternity until it chooses otherwise beloveds."

Light Prevails Eternally!

And It Is So

Amen

~ o ~

* Author's Note: If you are uncertain that you, your client or loved one is suffering a Demon affliction we may be contacted to provide a confirming Diagnostic Reading at: http://guidelights.org See the **Services Offered** page to request a Diagnostic Reading with an email summarizing the symptoms to: SoulFreedomRise@gmail.com

Glossary

Akashic: The Akashic Records are the thoughts, emotions and wisdom of all souls including their past, present, and probable future. The Library of the Akashic is where all souls' records are stored in higher frequency realms of consciousness.

Anorexia: An emotional disorder characterized by an obsessive desire to lose weight by refusal or inability to eat.

Ascended Master: It is humankind's soul evolvement to achieve Ascended Mastery through eternity. When a soul's purpose is to achieve Ascended Mastery in its one earth lifetime, he/she is guided through incredible strife to achieve Self Mastery. The purpose of this is to be an example to the world for the highest good of all.

Astral: 1) *Common:* Of or relating to a supposed nonphysical realm of existence to which various psychic and paranormal phenomena are ascribed, and in which the physical human body is said to have an etheric counterpart. 2) *Soul Freedom Series:* The astral realm is as an atmospheric field of consciousness in the spirit realm surrounding the earth and the universe. It is a field of travel between material worlds. It is also used to temporarily house human and alien soul spirits that become lost or stuck in the death transition between planets and the Spirit Realm.

Dimension: Earth is three-dimensional, the Astral realm is fourth dimensional, the Spirit Realm is fifth dimensional. There may be many Spheres of consciousness within a dimensional realm.

Divination: The practice of seeking knowledge of the future or the unknown by supernatural or intuitive means.

Elohim: God/Goddess's Creator Angels (mini God's).

Entity: Used in the context of this book refers to a Spirit being without a physical body of its own. A Spirit soul personality.

Esoteric: Spiritual topic.

Etheric body: The "human energy field", a souls Spirit body.

Illuminati: A secret society of people believed to be of very dark intent controlling the earth politically and financially in order to rule the world.

Implants: Implants are most commonly etheric mind control devices. They are meant to trigger our DNA and neurological systems that cause us to experience hallucinations, suicidal thoughts, taunting audible voices, etc. See *Entity Attachment Removal - Soul Freedom vol* 3 for specific help and free removal!.

Law of Attraction (LOA): The Law of Attraction is the law that positive or negative thoughts bring positive or negative experiences into a person's life. Positive = Good or high vibration. Negative = Bad or low vibration.

Mandala: A spiritual and ritual symbol in Hinduism and Buddhism used for meditation, (to achieve positive effects).

Medulla Oblongata: Indented hollow at the back of the head, top of neck and base of the skull.

Possession: State of taking over complete control of a persons' soul, mind and body.

Reincarnation: The rebirth of a soul in a new body.

Satanic: Demonic, extremely evil or wicked, diabolical and fiendish.

Shaman: A person having access to, and influence in, the world of good Spirits that are accessed with the purpose of divination and healing for the Earth and humanity.

Shape Shift: The ability of a human or spirit entity to change one's self into that of an animal or other type of being.

Soul: The spiritual or immaterial part of a human being regarded as immortal and retaining all soul records throughout the souls eternity.

Soul Fragment: When a human being is greatly traumatized a piece of the soul may fragment and stay energetically stuck at the scene of the trauma.

Soul Retrieval: A healer working in the world of Spirit retrieves a fragment of another's soul to reintegrate it to a return of self wholeness.

Sphere: Spiritual level of consciousness with Sphere 1 being the darkest/lowest.

Spirit Releasement Therapists: (SRT) Treatment coined by William J Baldwin PH.D. who trains medical and mental health professionals to heal clients from entity attachments and possessions by removing the invading entities.

Spirit: Author's definition: The God/Goddess life force that enlivens and moves with the soul consciousness and body as one.

Trapped Energy: Traumatic events cause souls to fragment and freeze the event of trauma into constant replay. The soul piece (fragment) becomes what is called trapped energy which can be felt throughout time until the soul emotion is healed or the soul fragments are returned to the soul. This happens to individuals as well as groups of individuals, such as in wartime.

Vibration: Vibration is the emanation of consciousness (as energy) in varying degrees of light or dark. How we think, eat and behave is impressed upon the personal energy that we radiate (vibrate).

Walk-In: Prior to birth a new soul agrees to a soul swap out with a spiritually enlightened being at an agreed upon point in their life. The purpose of this is to affect significant change at pivotal times in Earth's history for the highest good of all.

Witchcraft: Author's definition: A practice of creating magic spells to affect a person's life or that of another for good or for evil.

Bibliography

*Note: Books on the subjects of Spirit Release Therapy and Demons are included in the bibliography as research reference material only. I do not *necessarily* recommend or agree with their ideas, statements or practices.

Anatomy of the Spirit - The Seven Stages of Power and Healing by Caroline Myss, PhD

Arcturian Songs of the Masters of Light by Patricia Pereira

Autobiography of a Yogi by Paramahansa Yogananda

The Book of Knowledge: The Keys of Enoch® by J.J. Hurtak 1977

The Celestine Prophecy by James Redfield

Close Encounters of the Possession Kind by William J Baldwin, PhD

The Complete Ascension Manual - How to Achieve Ascension in This Lifetime by Joshua David Stone, Ph.D

The Dream Book - Symbols for Self Understanding by Betty Bethards

Emissary of Light: A Vision of Peace by James F. Twyman

Exploring Your Past Lives (1976) by Bryan Jameison

Entity Attachment Removal - Self-Help Procedure - The ABC of Releasing Spirit Attachments for Do It Yourselfers – Soul Freedom Series Vol 3 by Rise' Harrington and Bryan Jameison

Family of Light: Pleiadian Tales and Lessons in Living by Barbara Marciniak

A Field Guide to Demons - Theories, Fallen Angels, and Other Subversive Spirits by Carol K. Mack and Dinah Mack (Interesting reading but I, Rise' Harrington, believe most of this book is based only on myth).

Guide Lights - Attune to Your Angels and Spirit Guides - Begin to Heal Your Life and Move Towards Your Soul Purpose by Rise' Harrington

Heal Your Body – The Mental Causes for Physical Illness and the Metaphysical Way to Overcome Them by Louise Hay

Healing Lost Souls - Releasing Unwanted Spirits from Your Energy Body by William J Baldwin, PhD

The Highly Sensitive Person's Survival Guide: Essential Skills for Living Well in an Overstimulating World (Step-By-Step Guides) by Ted Zeff and Elaine N. Aron

Left To Tell - Discovering God Amidst the Rwandan Holocaust by Immaculee Ilibagiza

Love Without End – Jesus Speaks by Glenda Green

The Power of Now by Eckhart Tolle

The Ptaah Tapes: Transformation of the Species by Jani King and P'Taah

Radical Forgiveness – Making Room for the Miracle by Colin C. Tipping

Reincarnation – The Four Factors - Soul Freedom Series Vol 1 by Rise' Harrington and Bryan Jameison

Repelling Demons - The Loving Way to Heal Ourselves and Our World - Soul Freedom Vol 2 by Rise' Harrington and Bryan Jameison

The Search for Past Lives (2002) by Bryan Jameison

Shamanism for Beginners by James Endredy

Siddhartha by Hermann Hesse

Songs Of Malantor: The Arcturian Star Chronicles Volume Three by Patricia L. Pereira and Sue Mann

Soul Retrieval – Mending the Fragmented Self by Sandra Ingerman

The Unquiet Dead – A Psychologist Treats Spirit Possession by Dr. Edith Fiore

Website: www.DivineTruth.com by AJ Miller (AJ discusses Lost Soul Entity Attachment in videos throughout his website). The term he uses for spirit attachments is "over cloaking".

You Are Psychic – The Art Of Clairvoyant Reading and Healing by Debra Lynne Katz

Biography

------------ ~ * ~ ------------

About the Authors

Rise' (Reese) Harrington wrote her first book, *Guide Lights - Attune to Your Angels and Spirit Guides* to document the path that she developed in response to the internal presence and attack of dark forces throughout most of her young and adult life. Her life challenges included the uphill struggle with birth and trauma entity attachments, identity confusion, childhood sexual molestation and a Demonic possession attempt. The path that she was able to develop with the assistance of her Angels and spirit guides brought resolution of her own entity attachments as she rose from the darkness into the light, steadily growing vibrationally through the years beyond reach of the dark and Demonic factors. Her written material is expanded by the shared experience of thousands of people from her readers and Mediumship practice.

Rise's extensive experience in the corporate world in the documentation of procedures has resulted in a very effective procedural style manual for self-help healing. This, her second book is the popular Entity Attachment Removal - Self-Help Procedure - The ABC of Releasing Spirit Attachments for Do It Yourselfers. The culmination of these two books makes her an effective spiritual mentor and healer for people at all levels to raise themselves vibrationally in like manner and begin to evolve into their highest expressions of soul self.

Rise' received higher metaphysical instruction and guidance from her Angels, Spirit Guides and the Ascended Masters. She has since become merged with her Monadic higher self soul group of 35 other members and is now the earth-based spokesperson of this group called Andrameda. Soul mate Dorgeck co-authors her books under his original incarnation author name, Bryan Jameison.

Rise' has practiced mediumship focused on assisting the Lost Soul population for 20+ years. In 2013 she began offering Diagnostic Readings for Lost Soul Entity Haunting, Attachment and Demonic Possession with recommended treatments. All services are listed on the website.

http://guidelights.org/servicesoffered.html□

Rise's spiritual life path has been greatly influenced by 20 years of largely career related world travels to the Far East, Europe and Egypt.

She is a professional Medium and Minister of the Universal Life Church. She was raised in Los Gatos, California and now resides in San Diego County California.

Email Contact: soulfreedomrise@gmail.com
Web: http://guidelights.org

YouTube Channel
https://www.youtube.com/user/guidelights7

Bryan Jameison

May 8, 1933 - December 2, 2002

Born and raised in Chicago in May 1933 as James S. Lewis, he worked and wrote under the pseudonym Bryan Jameison. He later had his name officially changed to the latter.

Long acclaimed as a Master Past-Life regressionist, Bryan is internationally recognized as a true pioneer in the field of past-life therapy. After creating his own non-hypnotic method of past-life regression in 1968, he went on to facilitate more than 25,000 regressions and train nearly 2,000 others to become past-life regressionists in the United States, Canada and Western Europe.

Made in the USA
Middletown, DE
20 August 2023

37022495R00050